Root of the Matter

Sharnnell Spivey

Copyright © 2024 Sharnnell Spivey

All rights reserved.

ISBN: 978-1-7379162-2-2

DEDICATION

To my daughter who is going through the stage of finding herself. Remember, who you were then is who you are now. Your strength, courage, beauty and love for life is the same. Things happen in our lives that we will never understand, but in the mist of it, we must remember who we are and what we stand for.

CONTENTS

	Acknowledgments	i
1	Precious Jewel	1
2	Ruth the Abolitionist	21
3	1st Moon	37
4	3rd Moon	47
5	5th Moon	55
6	Discovery	67
7	Confirmation	93
	About the Author	103

ACKNOWLEDGMENTS

To anyone who is having a hard time in life not understanding which way to go or what to do. To those who questioned themselves asking why they were placed on this earth. THIS IS FOR YOU! May you realize that you are not lost but your true self just needs to be discovered from within!

Precious Jewel

I was sitting on my mother's couch in my green and black pajama's strolling through my phone. My birthday is tomorrow, and my mom insisted on having me over even though it's a Thursday.

My Mom was in the kitchen finishing my birthday dinner which consist of all my favorite, Jambalaya with beef sausages, chicken dumplings, banana pudding and Hawaiian sweet rolls. My stomach continued to growl waiting for it all to get done.

"It's the birthday girl!" My baby sister Aurora said walking into the living room.

"Let's party!" Amariah said walking in behind her.

"No" I replied not even looking their way. My sisters were very extra when it came to, well, just about everything. As the oldest, they looked up to me, but I constantly distance myself from them due to the age difference. Even with that, they still somehow convinced me into moving with them.

"Live a little" Aurora said, sitting on the other end of the couch.

"Right, you can't go in your room and lock your door here," said Amariah.

"I still have a room here, it just doesn't have a lock on it" I responded, and they both stuck their tongues out at me. I shook my head.

"Alright my beautiful princesses, dinner is ready" Mom said from the dining room. She'd already set the table.

"Yes, about time" Amariah said jumping up.

"No ma'am, you know better than to come to the table without washing your hands." Mom said and Amariah swiftly turned around and walked to the bathroom.

I waited until they both washed their hands before going to wash mine. After, I walked to the table and sat down. As usual, my mom had prepared all our plates but kept extras on the table just in case. My Mom bowed her head, said grace and we dug in.

"So, Jewel, you're turning the big 30, what are you doing for you birthday?" Mom asked.

"Oh, I don't know, I didn't have any plans on celebrating it" I responded.

"Why not?"

"I don't know, I just…don't" I lowered my head, I didn't want to talk about it. I didn't want my mom to know how sad I still was that we were now sitting at the table with an empty chair. I begin moving my food around on my plate as the memory of the day my mother came home and told me that my dad was gone.

"Jewel, hold your head up. You are much too beautiful to have your head hanging down."

"Yes ma'am"

"Is this about your father not being able to be here with you?" She asked but I didn't respond. "I know you miss your dad, and he is always here with you in spirit, but you cannot stay stuck in the past. You know he wouldn't want that for you or any of us. Dad is gone physically, and we cannot hear his voice, experience his touch or see him smile but spiritually he is always around, watching, making sure we're okay"

"I know Mom, it's just, hard."

"I know, grief takes time. You are free to feel sad, mad, angry whatever you feel you are entitled to it; just don't stay there too long because it can become something else, alright?"

"Okay."

"I don't want to cry, let's change the subject. Mom, what did you do for your 30th birthday?" Aurora asked.

"Oh, I had fun, it was one of the best birthdays I've had. We went painting, out to eat, to a play, stayed at the hotel and had a girl's night and then to end it all we played whirly ball"

"Whirly ball? What's that?" Amariah asked.

"It's like bumper cars, but you have a net and you're driving around trying to get the ball into the hoop. Any and every one can bump into you or knock your ball out of your net. It was fun; my cheeks were hurting so bad that day from laughing."

"Oh, that sounds fun. Aurora, we need to do that one day."

"I don't know if they still have it, but I'm sure you'll find something similar if they don't."

We all continued to talk about fun things we could do, well mainly them, I stayed quiet for the most part. Sounds like my mom had a great 30th birthday, I want to do the same, but I just feel...I don't know. I really don't know how to feel right now. After dinner, my sisters went to their room and before I could go to mine, my Mom called me over to her.

"I'm so glad you came over to spend a little time with me" she said hugging me.

"Me too Mom" she let go of the embrace and held my face in her hands.

"I know you feel like you lost of piece of yourself, but you have to remember who you are. You can't stay in this sunken place for long."

"What if I don't know who I am?" She let go, walked over to the cabinet in the dining room and pulled out a box.

"This, is for your birthday so don't open it until tomorrow."

"What is it?"

"It's a family necklace, passed down to everyone, on their 30th birthday. It's really a tradition and I think it's perfect timing for you. In the box you'll also find letters from everyone who wore the necklace on their 30th birthday and how they felt afterwards."

"What is it, magic or something?"

"Now you know I don't do magic, but I will say, we are spiritual beings having a physical experience and once we remember that our bodies house a spirit, and that spirit is our connection to God. We can see things differently, that's why I tell you girls, you must have your own spiritual encounter with God, to know that God is real for yourselves. You can't go off what people tell you."

"You always gave us the faith version and Dad gave up the spiritual version."

"And now that's he's gone, I will give you both. Your Dad and I decided long ago that we would teach both to you and it was up to you, what you do with the knowledge we instill." I took a deep breath.

"That was deep."

"Too deep?"

"No, I guess it was right on time."

"Good," she said and kissed my forehead. "Let me put this food up and get to bed."

"I got it Mom."

"Are you sure?"

"Yes."

"Thank you," she smiled.

"You're welcome."

I sat my phone down on the couch and begin cleaning up the dining room table. The food was already in Tupperware, all I had to do was put the top on and put it in the fridge. She'd also already cleaned the dishes, expect the plates and silverware we used. She like to clean while cooking, she always taught us that it was easier to keep the kitchen cleaner that way.

After I was done, I grabbed my phone and the box, then headed to my room. My Mom kept the house we grew up in so we could always have our own space any time we needed to come home.

Closing the door behind me, I went over to look in the mirror before getting into bed. My hair was long, and I like to keep my hair in natural hairstyles, barely putting heat to it. Today, it was just in a ponytail but still fluffed out in the back. I stared in the mirror, assessing my caramel skin tone, my nose, and almond shaped eyes. We all were the same complexion except Mom and Amariah, they were more of a coco brown. Dad always told me that the eyes where the key to the soul, and my soul must have been sad because my eyes were.

Breaking the trace, I was in, I laid on my bed, grabbed my phone and begin playing games on it. Before I knew it, it was 1 in the morning and I decided that was enough, I'd go to bed, but before doing that I grabbed the box my Mom gave me and opened it. I pulled about the necklace that contained a crystal, hanging from a silk thread. The crystal was wrapped in copper wire; almost caged. Then I pulled out a piece of paper that was laminated; that read:

"To the next family member, Happy 30th Birthday to you. We wish you the best on your journey of discovery. We all go through an identity stage; some will find themselves early and others will continue searching for who they are. This Kyanite crystal will help you put some things into perspective.

On the day of your 30th birthday and the day after, wear this necklace as well as when you sleep.

May you find, what you are searching for."

Strange, I thought. Under the paper, was a smaller box that contained letters, I'm guessing ones my mother described to me. Since it was already late, I put everything back in the box, placed it on the nightstand next to my bed and fell asleep.

The next morning, my Mom made us breakfast and then we grabbed our things and headed home. I made it home first and assumed, my sisters were out shopping as always before coming home.

With the day off and it being a Friday, I just wanted to sit around the house and relax but I knew my sisters weren't going to let that happen. After I put on my lounge wear, I sat on my bed and turned on the TV. As I flipped thought the channels, my phone continued to received notifications, which I'm sure were birthday texts, I ignored most of them, I would respond later; then my phone started ringing.

"Hello" I said answering the phone.

"HAPPY BIRTHDAY!!" my best friend, Sara, said yelling in my ear.

"Thank you."

"So, what are we doing?"

"I don't know, I really don't feel like doing anything."

"Oh no, you're coming out, I'm not trying to hear it."

"Ugh."

"I'm about to make plans, love you, goodbye," she said before hanging up.

I rolled my eyes, I seen this coming but still felt indifferent. Suddenly I remembered the necklace, maybe wearing it will somehow increase my excitement. So, I got up, grabbed the box from my dresser, pulled the necklace out and put it on. It was beautiful and polished, I loved it.

"Hey, hey," Amariah said as she knocked on the door and walked in the room while I was in the mirror. "Time to get ready."

"Ugh, for what?"

"Your birthday of course. We already booked a booth at your favorite lounge, so get dressed because the streets of New Orleans calls."

"Tell New Orleans I'm not home, or better yet just hang up."

"Girl, don't make me pull you out of that bed."

"Ugh," I said again before pulling the cover over my head.

"What's going on?" I heard Aurora come in and ask.

"Jewel thinks she's staying in the house today," said Amariah.

"HA! No way sis, so you might as well get up." I groaned and didn't move. The room grew silent and next thing I knew, Aurora and Amariah jump on me together yelling, "sister love!"

"Oh, my goodness! You two are like bed bugs." I said pushing them off me.

"The good kind, or the bad kind?" Amariah asked sarcastically.

"Out!" I pointed to the door.

"Okay, okay we're leaving but we're expect you to be dressed by 6, otherwise we'll jump on you again."

"Out!" I said again and laughed.

"Alright, alright" Aurora said putting her hands up in surrender and they both walked out of my room.

I don't understand why I can't sit in my room and mope all day. It's my birthday, I should be able to do what I want. I guess they're just trying to help but I'm still not in the mood for it. I looked at the clock and it was 10 in the morning. I was still tired from the night before, so I laid back down and slept 2 more hours.

When I woke up, I noticed a serving cover sitting on my nightstand. When I lift it up, I saw a grill cheese sandwich cut diagonally and a few pieces of fruit; strawberries, grapes and oranges. Next to the plate was a cooled cup of apple juice. I grabbed that first, sipping it and bringing life back into my body. I got up, grabbed my food tray from across the room, put my food on it and begin eating. When I was done, the bathroom and shower were much needed.

After my shower, I put my robe on and embraced that fact that, I do need to get out of the house enjoy myself.

"Hey Alexa, play Beautiful by Mali Music," I said. As the music played, I brushed my teeth, cleaned my face, and put my make up on. After, I put on some plain jeans and a shirt. It was too early to get dressed for the night.

"Knock, Knock" I heard Aurora at the door.

"Come in."

"Hey, are you ready?" she asked.

"I thought you guys said 6 o'clock."

"For dinner yes, but it was pushed back to 8 pm."

"So, why do I need to be ready?"

"Oh, we're taking you shopping, new outfit and shoes."

"Is all of the that really necessary?"

"No but Sara requested it, and I thought it was a great idea. So, get your I.D. we are treating you today and um you might want to grab some gum. You just let that toothpaste sit in your mouth and fester." She said placing her hand over her nose.

"Okay, get out."

"Don't get mad at me, I'm trying to help you out. Oh, no." She said wide eyed and dramatically.

"What?"

"Is this why you're still single, because you have halitosis?"

"Girl, get out of my room" I said pushing her out the door.

"Okay, see you in the car in 10 minutes, love you, goodbye," she managed to say before I shut my room door. I then placed my hand in front of my face, checking my breath. "Ew, she may get on my nerves, but she was right, let me grab some gum." I said heading over to my dresser where my purse sat.

Since they were treating me to everything, I just packed a few essentials in a smaller, over the shoulder bag. I checked my face one more time and headed downstairs. Once downstairs, I looked around for my sisters and didn't see them, so I headed outside to the car. I was right, there both sitting in Amariah's truck; I walked over and got in the front passenger seat, Amariah smiled.

"Yeah, are you ready?" she asked.

"No" I responded.

"Oh, don't be like that, we're going to have fun, promise."

She backed out of the driveway, and we headed to the clothing store.

"So what store were you thinking?" I asked.

"Maybe Saks," Amariah responded.

"Have you lost your mind?"

"What's wrong with Saks?"

"It cost an arm and a leg and maybe a toe."

"Well, what store would you like to get your outfit from?"

"Trashy Diva," Aurora laughed.

"Jewel, please explain the difference between the two because the price range is about the same."

"Culture."

"Okay, you have a point. Trashy Diva, here we come!" She said and parked a little further down from the store, as the street was packed.

When we walked in, we were each greeted and giving a glass of champagne. The staff seated us in a secluded section of the store where I'd be able to try on clothes in private. The room formed a circle with a circular couch, 3 changing rooms in front of it and a tall wide mirror that gave us a full view.

"Geez, what great service. It's like they knew we were coming," I said sitting down.

"Oh, they did, I scheduled this a month ago," said Amariah and I heard Aurora laugh.

"How did you schedule this a month ago when you first said that we were going to Saks?"

"Oh, I lied," she said sitting next to me.

"Did you know?" I asked Aurora.

"Of course, you think we don't know our sister."

"Whatever," I said to both and then took a sip of my champagne.

"Are you ready?" A woman said as she walked in with a rack of dresses. "We've picked out the best ones based on your taste in clothing. I'll leave this here and let you get to it."

"Thank you," we said in unison.

I stood up, walked over to the rack in amazement looking through all the dress.

"Are you going to put your drink down?" asked Aurora.

"Exactly, because we're only paying for one dress, maybe two but don't spill champagne on nothing." Said Amariah.

"I'm not going to spill it." I responded.

"I'm not taking no chances, hand it over" Amariah said holding her hand out.

I gave her a side glare and walked the glass over to her, then went back over to the dresses. They were all my style, surprisingly, my sisters did good. They are quite annoying, but I appreciate their efforts.

"Well, let's get it!" Amariah said excitingly.

I grabbed a few dresses and began the process of trying them on. It was fun, laughing, joking and parading around in these beautiful dresses was so much fun. I would pose, putting one hand on one hip and the other, on my head as if I'd fainting as they continuously snapped pictures.

"What about this one?" I said walking out of the dressing room to the mirror and examining myself. "Ooo, I really like this one." I said looking over the black dress with yellow trim, draped perfectly over me.

"I love the bow on the back," Aurora said.

"Me too, I think this will do."

"Alright, we got the dress! Now it's time for shoes!" Amariah said in excitement. I laughed; I can't believe I almost missed out on sister time.

We paid for the dress, went shoe shopping then headed back home to get ready. I was all smiles and laughs, until I was fully dressed. Looking in the mirror, trying to figure out who was staring back at me. She is me and I am her, but we are strangers. How is that possible?

I looked down at the family necklace I was still wearing. "I hope this helps." I said to myself. I closed my eyes and took a deep breath before grabbing my crossbody purse and heading downstairs.

"Hey sexy lady." Amariah said when she seen me. I smiled, took a slow turn, and then posed. "Now that's what I'm talking about! Get it sis!"

"I'm trying, I'm trying. Y'all ready?"

"Waiting on Aurora, you know she takes forever."

"I beg your pardon, beauty takes time." Aurora said walking into the room with an all-white bodycon, short sleeve dress.

"Girl who do you think you are in all this white?" Amariah asked.

"Same person you think you are in all that red." Aurora responded.

"Alright, understood." They begin to laugh. These girls are crazy. "One shot before the road."

We each grabbed a glass and took a shot before headed outside. There was a limo waiting for us. I stood shocked for a minute as I watched them excitingly run to it. My best friend was already in the limo waiting for us. We talked and laughed on the way to the club. Dance until we could dance anymore then headed home. We dropped my best friend off, making sure she arrived home safely and us too. As we slowly walked into the door, tired from all the dancing and a little intoxicated; I made sure to lock the door behind us.

"Alright, I'm going to bed. Thanks for the fun!" I said slowly making it up to my room. They did not respond but I did see a thumbs up, guess they're as tired as I was.

I kicked my shoes off at my door and walked into my bathroom to take my makeup off. As I was finished cleaning my face, I saw her again, the stranger in the mirror. I was too tired to analyze myself so after putting on my pajamas; I walked over to my bed and practically fell into it.

Making myself comfortable under my comforter, I drifted off to sleep in a matter of seconds.

Ruth the Abolitionist

"Ruth! Ruth! Quick! They sold her," I heard a woman say shaking me out of my sleep. I jumped up, unable to catch my breath. I could see figures moving around, waving their hands for me to come near but my eyes hadn't adjusted yet. Everything was still so blurry. I assumed it was Aurora, so I got out of the bed and headed toward the doorway where she was standing. Rubbing my eyes, trying to clear my vision but on the other side of the door was not the hallway of our home, but I outside. I was outside. The smell of dust and dirt filled my nose, and I began to cough.

"Ruth, didn't you hear what I said, they sold Momma," the voice said again, and I was finally able to get a good look at who was talking to me, and it wasn't Aurora. I stood there speechless and before I could fix my mouth to say anything I heard a woman screaming from a distance. I looked around and saw a black woman, bound by her wrist with a thick rope, tied to the back of a wagon. I could see a crowd begin to form as the young lady who'd called me Ruth, ran off the porch to the wagon crying.

I couldn't breathe, what was happening? What kind of dream was this? My vison began to get blurry again as I tried to understand what was going on. I placed my hand on my head, trying to compose myself but it was no use. Seeing people try to get to the woman on the wagon and being hit with a whip, like, like they were, can't be. No, no, no this can't be true. Slaves? Are they slaves, I said softly to myself before collapsing.

I remember letting out a groan as I slowly opened my eyes. My vision was still blurry, but I could see someone sit by my side and I felt a warm towel being placed on my head.

"Ugh, what's going on?" I said in a groggy voice trying to sit up.

"No, lay down. Let me fetch you some water" the same young lady said who'd woke me up prior to me fainting. Once my vision was clear, I saw her smile then walk over to the fireplace. I watched as she grabbed a long wooden spoon and used it to scoop out water that was in a pot over the fireplace. After putting everything back in its place, she walked over to me with the cup. "Here, you'll feel better after you drink this, promise" I didn't protest, I sat up, took the cup and begin drinking the water which seemed to contain salt. Then I put my hand on my head, it was still hurting so I laid back down.

"Who's Ruth?" I asked softly. The woman looked at me funny then placed the back of her hand to my forehead.

"No fever," she said.

"Why would I have a fever?"

"Think you would, if you don't know who you is" She said with a confused look on her face.

"What? My name is Jewel."

"Our daddy named ya Ruth. That's ya name." She said firmly.

Before I could ask anything else a young Caucasian woman bust through the door and lounged at me with open arms.

"Oh Ruth, I'm so sorry they sold yo Momma. Must have given you such a fright to make you fall like that."

"Was a shock on us all, Ms. Sarah. Ruth's not herself after that nasty fall."

"Well, what's wrong with her?"

"I don't know really, but I can fetch the doctor to come look at her."

"You do that MaryAnn"

"Yes, ma'am." Ms. Sarah turned back to me with a smile.

"Okay Ruth, I'll give you three days to get back on your feet and get to work, otherwise we won't have no use for you" she said to me with a smile as if it was a compliment. I just stared at her, assessing the situation then looked at MaryAnn who stood a distance from us with her hands folding in front of her apron. Her head was slight lowered, and she didn't move until Ms. Sarah finally left out of the...cabin, I think it was.

"Stay here," MaryAnn said before leaving out of the cabin as well.

I was confused, where was I, when was I? I must be dreaming because none of this makes any sense. Am I trapped in a dream, or should I say horrible nightmare? I just laid there trying to figure out how I was going to get away from these crazy people. If I could even do that. If I'm stuck in a dream, during slavery, what consequences would I face trying to escape? Will it affect me in my waking life?

As I continued to question myself, MaryAnn walked back in with a tall black man, the same man I'd seen earlier reaching out for the woman in the wagon.

"Ruth! Ruth!" he said rushing to my side. I stared at him with confusion.

"See Papa. She says she don't know who she is. If she don't know who she is, then she don't know us."

"Fetch me some water MaryAnn." he said.

"Yes, sir," she said grabbing water from the same pot, along with a rag that looked more like a torn piece of cloth. The man dipped the rag in the water, rung it out and lightly patted my forehead with it. He then slowly turned and looked at MaryAnn, who without hesitation, left out of the cabin.

"Really don't need you getting sick. Folks believe you half dead, and they kill you or worse, sell you," he said.

"I'm not property." I responded, still tired and weak.

"As long as you a slave, then you is," he said as a matter of fact.

"Slave?" I said sitting up on my elbows. "I'm not a slave." Before he could respond, Mary Ann walked back into the cabin.

"I brought some medicine for Ruth," she said.

"Good, tend to her, hear?" he responded before walking out of the cabin.

MaryAnn walked close to me before speaking. "Daddy sure make a big fuss about you, don't he? Think he'd be fussing more about them selling Momma off." She continued to talk while dipping a rag in water and dabbing it across my forehead. I laid there, thinking, trying to make sense of things.

"You think he'll find her?" I asked.

"Well, if he has any sense, he'll stay put; but daddy don't have any sense." She laughed and I joined in with the slightly nervous laugh. "You though, what we gone do with you?"

"I don't know. I don't even know what going on, maybe if I had time…"

"Don't have time…" she begin to say but stopped when she heard children laughing loudly. "Oh no." I could see fear grow in her eyes before she dropped everything and ran outside. I slowly got up and ran behind her to the doorway to see what was happening.

There were two small children running, laughing, and playing. I watched as MaryAnn attempted to get their attention, standing five feet from the cabin calling their names, but they couldn't hear her over their laughter. I opened the door wider, stepping out on the porch. I didn't understand why she didn't just walk over there on her own, but I continued to watch MaryAnn try to get them to come over to her instead, I laughed at the sight. The children were chasing each other in circles, in an open area. I didn't see what the problem was.

My smile slowly began to disappear when I spotted a man riding a horse, getting closer to the children. The man looked angered as he rode the horse galloping across the field. I looked at MaryAnn who was now running towards the children. I left the porch and followed suit.

MaryAnn and the man arrived at the children at the same time. That's when the children finally looked up and noticed. She tried to grab them but was met with a whip that landed at her feet.

"Get back, get back I say." The man said forcing MaryAnn step backward; moving at least five feet from the children.

As I moved closer, I still couldn't see his face. The sun shined so bright only casting a shadow of him. I could see him circling the now frightened children still on the horse, wearing a cowboy hat. He drew back the whip and before I knew it, I ran, stood in front of the children, blocking my face. I lifted my left arm, using it as a shield to block the whip.

I yelled out in pain as the whip connected to my arm and wrapped around it. The pain sent a jolting feeling in my body and before I knew it, I yanked my arm back causing the whip to fly out of his hand. Everyone was in disbelief. Now comforting my arm, I heard the man jump off of the horse, his feet hitting the ground hard. Without a word he walked up to me and slapped me hard across the face.

"Have you lost your mind gal?" He asked.

Me? It was he who'd lost his mind. Holding the right side of my face I slowly turned around to face him but before I could react, MaryAnn grabbed me from behind.

"Forgive her, she's not feeling well." She said with worry in her voice.

"You get that gal together or I'll sell her just as fast as I sold your Momma."

"Yes, sir. Yes, sir." She responded with a bow and nod. He stared at me a little bit longer before climbing back on his horse and riding away.

I was angered, completely forgetting about my headache, and lash on my arm as the adrenaline ran through my body. I couldn't believe she would bow to him like that and not respond. Even with all the movies and shows I've seen about slavery; nothing compared to being here. To enduring the madness firsthand and everything felt so real. If this is a dream, then this is a nightmare.

"Come." I heard MaryAnn say, bringing me back to reality, back to the pain shooting in my arm and the warmth on my face.

I followed, cuffing my now split open left arm with my right arm. No one came to assist, instead they watched.

Watched as if I was taking a walk of shame as I went back to the cabin.

"Sit. Let me look at ya." She said examining my arm. "You must want those white folks to sell you off, so we never see you again." She said tending to my wound, cleaning the area, and then wrapping it in an off-white cloth. "Guess I'll be paying for your actions tonight."

"Tonight?"

"You really don't remember do you?" MaryAnn said annoyed.

"No"

"Guess, that's better; to forget. I'd love to forget all of this." She paused, recalling memories before finishing up the bandages. "I close my eyes and dream I'm free every time he touches me. Every time."

"Are you his…"

"Bed maid. What I wouldn't give to not remember. I don't know if it's a blessing or curse." This saddened me and I held my head down as if I was defeated. "Hold your head up, you're strong, stronger than anyone I know besides Momma. I don't want to lose you too, I can't." She said leaning her forehead against mine, taking a deep breath and soaking in the moment.

"Everything will be just fine. We'll get you better in no time and back in the house."

"What's my role?" I asked.

"Role?"

"What do I usually do...here?"

"You work in the house with me. You cook and clean and..." she paused before continuing. "Whatever is asked of ya."

"I can't do this!" I said putting my face in my hands.

"You can and you will. You won't have to do it much longer."

"What do you mean?"

"We're leaving."

"Leaving?"

"Yes, leaving. Better get your mind right because you're our leader, you're supposed to guide us north."

"To freedom?"

"Yes, where else? I can't wait to get there, I bet you the air taste different." She said with a smile.

"If I can't remember, how am I going to lead you?"

"The paper." She said in almost a whisper. "I saw Minty bring it to you before she left. If we follow it, we can make it out."

"Just you and me?"

"No, it's 'bout eight of us so far, Frank say, he not going. Say he scared on the count of them catching Charles, whooped him so bad, they had no use for him, so they shot him dead."

I shook my head in disbelief. What type of horrible dream is this? Okay God, you can wake me up now, I thought to myself, but I was still there. Still in that horrible nightmare.

"I have to leave. I'll send Abagail to check on you" MaryAnn said standing to leave.

"Abagail?" I asked.

MaryAnn just smiled slightly, rested her hand on my shoulder before turning and walking out of the cabin.

I sat there, waiting to be woken up from the nightmare or someone to walk in and tell me that this was a joke. A joke that went too far, but nothing…and no one came.

I took a deep breath and listened to the sounds around me. I could hear horses, wagons going by, some fast, some slow. I closed my eyes, focusing in on the sounds, getting familiar with them because if this is my new life. I need to know my new surroundings. If I don't talk, walk or behave myself in the proper manner, I won't make it. I won't live.

"Ruth!" I heard someone say startling me as they walked inside the cabin. She stopped right in the middle of the cabin and looked at me. "Are you…" she began to say as she took another step closer but stopped.

"Abagail?" I asked and she smiled, rushing over to me.

"You remember?"

"No. MaryAnn said you were coming." Her smile left her face just as quickly as it arrived.

"If you don't remember, that mean we on our own?" she asked.

"I…I…"

"Oh Ruth, I can't stay here, I just can't."

"MaryAnn, said something about a piece of paper."

"I have it here. Bets not pull it out." I nodded in agreement. "Five moons. Five days' time we will cross the River Jordan and with you being our agent, I know we in good hands. If I die, it'll be on free land." She said in the matter of a fact tone with a big smile on her face. I didn't speak, there was no need to. "I brought you some bread from the house." She said pulling out a cloth, when she unwrapped it, there was a piece of bread inside.

"Thank you." She nodded, patting my shoulder and then left. I notice between the interactions I've had so far, that they tend to speak more with gestures and eye contact than anything.

I examined the bread before taking a bite. It wasn't too hard, nor too soft, dry and contained very little flavor. I realized if I didn't drink water with it, I'd choke, so I got up and grabbed water from the pot. Making the bread bearable. I dipped in the water and then ate it.

As I sat and ate the bread, I thought to myself, this is crazy, I've heard stories, saw movies but I never thought I'd live the life. I don't know if I can do this, but I also can't abandon the promise I gave to them, which was hope. At the same time, how do I give them hope with I'm so lost and confused myself. I don't know this land, I don't even know what state I'm in right now but, I must find a way, I must. Whoever this Ruth person is, she made a promise that I must now keep.

Trying to piece everything together I said softly, I'm a slave, I'm supposed to lead people to freedom using a map by someone name Minty. Minty? I thought. Why does that name sound so familiar?

Hold on, Minty gave me the route, like Harriet, Moses of slaves, Minty? I thought. Well, that's messed up, I couldn't wake up in this place beforehand so I can actually meet her. "Stop" I said to myself, I need to focus. Today is day 1, and I know absolutely nothing about this place. I need to take my time and try to learn as much as possible. Learn my role, as well as how to help these people. I have to be honest with myself, I'm very sick to my stomach about being here but I'm here now so I might as well do what I have to do to survive.

Root of the Matter

1ˢᵗ Moon

As the day went on, people came in and out of the cabin checking on me to make sure I was okay. I only left the cabin to use to bathroom or outhouse. I continued to play sick, giving myself enough time to prepare mentally for the journey ahead.

After laying back down in the bed, MaryAnn came over with a steel bucket filled with water, reached in it and pulled out a cloth. After she rang out some of the water, she used the cloth to wipe my forehead as she softly sang, "Steal away, steal away, steal away to Jesus." I remember my mom and dad teaching that song to use when we were young.

"How is she?" The door swung open, and a man walked in. MaryAnn jumped to her feet, dusted her apron, and put her head down before speaking. He stood tall, white, and handsome but had an unfriendly look about him.

"Getting better sir." MaryAnn said.

"Good, less y'all work, less money I make. The first night she's well, you send her to me you understand."

"Yes sir."

I didn't respond, only watched the interaction between them. The exchange of words, the body moments, and the tense energy. He stared at me before turning and walking out, I could easily tell he was the slave owner. The other man I encountered, the one who'd hit me with the whip, seemed like he only worked for the family. Then it hit me, damaging my presence at night could only mean one thing, and I wasn't going to let that happen.

The door closed and MaryAnn stood there as we both listened to him walk away. You could hear the gravel as he walked. Once we no longer heard his footsteps, MaryAnn looked up at me, hands still folded in front of her.

"Fight." Were the words she said before leaving me all alone in my thoughts.

Fight, I thought. I really didn't have a choice. There was no room for tears, no room for symphony and definitely no room for errors. I was scared, terrified, if I'm being honest; but here, in this place, in this time, that was a sign of weakness. That weakness would do nothing but destroy hope and I couldn't let that happen.

Maybe I'll fall asleep and this whole thing will be over. I like this option better. I got as comfortable as I could, closed my eyes and quickly drifting off to sleep.

I slowly opened my eyes the next morning, hopeful that I was back home, back in my bed, back to my normal life.

"Oh, you've got to be kidding me." I said aloud. I was still there. I threw the blanket over my face to mask the frustrating scream that I couldn't hold in.

Isaac, my father in this time, walked in right after I let out the last scream.

"You likely kill me before my time with worry." He spoke.

"Sorry. I just don't know if I can do this." I responded.

"Don't let fear lead you. Remember, the dead trees will show you the way and I'll be right there."

"You're coming?"

"Of course. Survive or die trying. Come on, let's get something in your belly. Brought you some rice from the big house." I got up, walked over and sat and the table with my father. I didn't realize it at first but his mannerisms, and a few structures of his face.... he looked.... he looked like my actual father. "What's the matter?" He asked as I stared at him.

"Nothing."

"Okay, eat up. I'll be back to check on you." I nodded in agreement and began eating my rice. You could see the species that were grounded up and placed on top of it. It was much better than the bread, although it was slightly overcooked. The spoon was made of wood like the bowl. Nicely craved and wide, like a soup spoon.

As I examined the spoon, I got an idea. Wood, this spoon could be sanded and shaped into a weapon. Sharpened on the end, it can be a knife.

After I finished my breakfast, I stepped outside to walk the outhouse; dragging my feet along the ground, I kicked the rocks. I was looking for an odd, shaped rock for craving and I found one. I kicked it into the outhouse and once I was inside, I placed the rock in my dress, near my breast.

For two days I keep every other spoon brought to me and scaped away at little by little using the rock I'd found. The only person that noticed the spoons were missing was MaryAnn. She looked at me oddly every time she would take my bowl to have it cleaned, I didn't return the spoon. She knew I was up to something but never questioned me.

"Think it's time you help with a chore" MaryAnn suggested.

"Which one?" I asked.

"Come, help me with the basket" she said leaded me outside to an open area where clothing lines ran from one pole to the other. She stopped and turned towards me, "Can you pin these here cloths up?"

"Yes," I said bending down and grabbing the pure white sheets. My arm was still in a little pain, and I felt the reminder when I reached up to pin the cloth, stretching the skin on my arm.

The wound wasn't that bad just mainly sore. MaryAnn wrapped it up tight for me keeping the pressure on it so that the wound wouldn't reopen.

For hours, I was on my feet, in the sun, pinning up sheets. No breaks, no water, I was tired and dehydrated but I knew I couldn't move. I knew I couldn't leave to get a drop of water. Sweat was dripping down my forehead into my eyes. I continue to wipe the sweat away with my arm to keep my hands from getting dirty. When the basket was empty, I picked it up and carried it in front of me, two hands on each side. Walked it up to the big house, as they called it and placed it in a pile of baskets sitting at the back of the house.

Right before I turned around to walk back, the back door swung open and there he was again, smiling, looking at me as if I was a piece of meat.

"How long must I wait for you gal?" He asked, and I didn't know how to respond. It felt like a summons, and it made me feel dirty. "What's the matter, cats got your tongue?" He teased as he walked down the steps in his boots towards me. I stepped back, not knowing what he'd do next, and he grabbed my arm, the injured one and I let out a painful cry. "Oh, I see you're not all healed up, guess I'll give you a day or so more" he said before grabbing my face and forcefully kissing me. I didn't kiss him back. When he was done, he pushed me away and I stumbled, almost falling. "Guess you better get back to work now, see you soon." He tipped his head forward and walked back into the house.

I was held my stomach, trying to catch my breath and trying not to throw up. I was disgusted and this action, this one action made everything feel surreal. Not the fact that I could taste the dirt in the air, not the whip hitting my arm but him putting his filthy lips on me. I wanted to scrub my entire body, I felt so dirty.

I hurried back to my cabin. Once I made it back, I threw up at the back of the cabin. The nerve, treating me like I was some kind of meat. I hate it here and I want out! Whatever I'm supposed to do, I need to do quickly and go home. No one should have to live like this, especially on a daily basis.

The image flashed into my mind, and I threw up again.

After the second time, I walked to the front of the cabin and went inside. I retrieved water from the pot still sitting about the fire and used it to rinse my mouth out, spitting the water on the logs that were in the fireplace.

Great, no toothpaste, I thought to myself.

"What are you doing?" MaryAnn asked catching me in the act. I hadn't heard her come in.

"I threw up." I said, looking at her with shame.

"So, you wet the logs we need for the fire?"

"Oh, I wasn't thinking…"

"The Lord just needs to strike me dead if you don't get your mind right," she threw her arms up and walked out only to come back with more wood and some leaves. "Here, dip these mint leaves in the water and rub them on your tongue, should help with the smell."

"Thank you," I said, still ashamed.

I watched as she switched the wet logs out for the dry ones.

"Can I help?" I asked.

"Naw, bets leave it to me, I think you've had enough today" Oh she was upset, and she had every right to be. I'd messed up today and although I'm not from this time, I should be more cautious, more aware of how things work around here.

I kept my distance, not wanting to upset her more. I undressed and laid down for bed. She did the same, laying on the other side bed. Night came, and I could hear the crickets chirping outside, but that was about it. No other sound, not even the wind. I was alone in the thoughts, wondering if I'll be ready when the time comes to leave? Do I have what it takes? What if I'm not strong enough? What if I'm not brave enough? What if we get caught? And so on, and so on. I shook my head removing my thoughts. I didn't have room for doubt, no room for being afraid nor second guessing myself. I needed to learn as much as I can in the little time that I have so that I can leave and take those I promised to safety with me.

I promised them. I kept saying in my head over and over, hoping that if I continued to hear it, it would knock the fear out of me and strength me more.

Root of the Matter

3rd Moon

As the days went on, I became curious. How long has our family been here, at this plantation, in America?

"Does he talk about the…old life?" I asked MaryAnn while she wiped down the table, she paused and slowly looked at me.

"Don't ask those kinds of questions" she responded.

"I just want to know…"

"You just finsta get us in trouble, that's what it is" she said.

"No MaryAnn, I can't remember everything, I just…I just want to know," she paused.

"Fine!" she said and walked over to sit close to me. She spoke softly, to make sure not be heard by others. "I will only say this once. We are Mbundu people, decedents of Queen Njinga. The Queen tried to protect us but when we were very young. Kambu, our brother, tried to fight back after his friend was taken, they killed him. When mother and father took us out to look for him, we were captured. I don't remember the ferry and I don't want to; I don't remember our real names or our language, but I do remember wondering free. I want to see that again. I've only tried to stay alive, do as I'm told, do what I must. I don't want to be touch by white men no more. I want my own man. My own life." She said clinching her fits to her chest and looking up. She then looked at me with anger. "Don't you go asked father any questions. No more of this talk. I see you, sister, I see you." She said with sincerely in her eyes.

She didn't say anything else after that just continued to clean.

I felt it all, everything she said to me, I felt her pain through her eyes.

"Now come on, let's get to the market." MaryAnn said reaching out to me. I grabbed her hand, and she bent down to grab two wooden woven baskets. She handed me one and we left out of the cabin, arms linked and walked to town.

We started on a dusty and rocky road, nothing but fields and trees until we reached town, and it was just like the movies. Everything rustic. I noticed MaryAnn lower her head as we approached the market, so I did the same, mimicking her.

I thought we would go to the front, but she instead led me to the back door. She knocked and stepped back, waiting for it to be answered. When it was, she didn't say anything, not a word, she only handed a tall white man a piece of paper in which he snatched it out of her hand and went back into the store.

Dogs is what came to my mind. Treated like dogs or maybe even worse. She didn't move and neither did I as we waited at the back door. It was strange. In movies I'd seen them go into the store and the clerk either watches or does the shopping for them. However, the feeling of being treated so low, hit me very differently than reading or watching it on screen. It was harsher, more degrading than another I'd ever experienced.

The first older man didn't return, instead, two younger ones, with smiles on their faces.

"Hey MaryAnn & Ruth, how y'all doing today?" One asked.

"Good sir," she responded.

That's good, I got y'all everything you need, just sat those baskets down and we'll filler up." Such joy, such happiness in his voice. We did as he asked, head still down, making sure not to make eye contact.

After the baskets were full, the same young man, walked closer to MaryAnn to whisper, "I put some of those sweet rolls in the basket that you like, right under the onions." He stepped back. "Alright na, you gals are all set."

"Thank you, sir," we said in union and MaryAnn did a small curtsy before we walked away. I didn't say anything not until we made it out of the town and were back on the dirty roads.

"Who was that man?" I asked.

"Ed, he sweet on me," she said still looking forward, I was looking at the ground.

"Are you sweet on him?" She laughed.

"What I look like being with a white man. Them white folks would string me up just thinking about it."

I didn't respond, because of the laugh. Was it because the question was funny or did, she laugh to keep from crying I couldn't tell.

"Keep your head low. Since you don't remember nothing, you don't need to see this."

I didn't know what she meant but I heard whimpering. Soft sobs and then a loud cry. The cry startled me, and I looked up in panic and saw…a woman and two young boys kneeling by a tree. A tree that we just passed, a tree that no longer had empty branches but there, on the branch, a man now hung.

My breathing became heavy as everything begin to spin.

"I told you not to look," MaryAnn said as she put her basket down and grabbed me, holding on to me as if she was holding on to life.

I was breaking down, slowing falling to the ground as I watch them cry over him. The cruelty, the pain, her cries, their cries, it was all too much so I begin shaking my head uncontrollable and covered my ears.

"Ruth! Ruth!" Her voice was distance even though she was right beside me. A slap across my face brought me back to reality, well this reality.

"Ruth, please, gather the food so we can head back, if were late, we might as well be hanging next to him."

I shook my head in the yes motion, and she helped me up. Dusting off our dresses and grabbing the baskets, we begin to walk again. This time, I put my head down and kept it down as we passed by the family.

My stomach was turning in complete knots, but I knew that there was nothing I could do. I couldn't be weak, I had to be strong, strong enough to get them out of the place. Strong enough to fight if I have to.

Once we arrived back to the big house, MaryAnn took both baskets inside and told me to go lay down for a while. I nodded and walked away still in a daze, still haunted by the cries, still haunted by the sight of a dead man hanging. I felt like I was trapped in a twilight zone. This world is cruel, this time is cruel.

I grabbed a hold of the cabin as everything begin to spin again before throwing up. How? How did they live like this daily? How did they grow old and generation after generation suffer so long? I cannot be weak, I must fight for them, I must keep my promise and lead them to freedom, there is no way, no way in hell, I am backing out of this! I will fight for them! I will succeed! I said to myself as a reassurance, and I meant every word!

I went inside the cabin and cleaned myself up. I think I was done for today. MaryAnn walked through the door.

"Told 'em, you wasn't feeling well and needed to lay down but I need to be to the field. Rest sister." She said tapping my shoulder and leaving as quickly as she came.

Good! This would give me more time. More time to plan out everything. I had about four wooden spoons that I'd craved into weapons. I thought about rocks but the weight of carrying them would slow us down. I decided to make a few arrows instead and mentally prepare for the escape.

My mind was still so shocked, so hurt and confused but I needed to succeed and in order to do that, I needed a clear head. I need to relieve myself of the painful thoughts that continue to cycle in my mind. I couldn't imagine what anyone else was thinking during this time as I alone have only encountered this insane life for a few days. I wanted out and I wanted out, NOW!

There was nothing, nothing that was going to hold me back, nothing that was going to stand in my way. I am going to lead them. I WILL lead them and no one and I mean NO ONE will stop me!

Root of the Matter

5th Moon

Today was the day we were going to run, to get away. As the day went on, we stood in the corn fields collecting crop when they broke out in song:

"Wade in the water, wade in the water, children, wade in the water. God's gonna trouble the water.

See that host all dressed in white, God's gonna trouble the water. The leader looks like the Israelite. God's gonna trouble the water.

See that band all dressed in red, looks like the band that Moses led.

If you don't believe I've been redeemed, just follow me down to Jordan's stream"

A farewell song, something to comfort us on our journey. The words and the melody were so calming to me. I used my breathing to calm myself and prepare for what was to come.

Night came and we all gathered in our cabins waiting for the signal. I'd wrapped all the spoons in a cloth and placed them in my pocket. I insisted on wearing the men's breeches to move around easier. I managed to make a very quiver and strapped that to my back, placing the two arrows I made inside of it.

We waited silently before we heard the drums. Our hearts pounding but ready to take this chance.

We quietly walk out of the cabin slowly moved across the rocks to keep from making noise. Once we were on the grass, we took off running towards the woods. MaryAnn led them as I ran behind them trying to get to make sure no one was left behind.

Although Isaac was older, he kept us with us. We made it to the first stop, a barn house. We stopped to rest, eat, and collect ourselves.

"How long we gon rest?" Abigail asked.

"Just a little while, we must keep going" I said.

"But my feet hurt."

"We left, and either they're going to bring a us back to kill or sell us." They all looked around at one another. No one rather go back, we all rather keep going, keep moving.

I could see that they needed a break. Daytime was amongst us. I looked at the paper Minty left me and it showed a door on ground near the barn, a root cellar.

"Stay here," I told them as I got up and walked around the barn looking for the door. I found it, closer to the woods but it was there, covered in leaves and sticks. I begin removing the sticks when Isaac came up behind me to assist. He didn't speak just helped me move them. Once we were done, I said, "Get them, we can rest here, safely." He nodded and headed off.

By time he'd returned with them, I'd opened the hatch door a horrible smell hit me. Before walking down the steps, I used my shirt to cover my nose. A dead animal is what it was.

"Wait, let me remove it," Isaac said, and I nodded in agreement, running back up the stairs to throw up.

"Too much for you," MaryAnn said with laughter.

"Shut up," I responded after catching my breath.

Isaac pulled three rabbits and two squirrels out of the cellar. That was evidence within itself, that smell would have alerted anyone. Isaac walked a ways before tossed the dead animals and returning. In that time, we waited, allowing the smell to clear.

"Okay, we can't rest long but we must rest before continuing. We are close." I said and they agreed.

"I will stand watch," Isaac suggested.

"No, you must rest too," I responded.

"No, my child, we must not sleep too long, I will wake you all when it's time." I nodded in agreement, and we gathered in the cellar, sitting in a circle with our backs to each other, leaning on one another and at the same time, protecting each other.

"Hey, hey it's time," I heard and felt a nudge as I opened my eyes. Isaac began to wake everyone else up. I headed up the steps. MaryAnn somehow was already awake, standing outside, looking around.

"It's beautiful, isn't it," she said as I approached.

"Very."

"I hope it remains as beautiful to me as it does now."

"Even more, I sure," I said as I grabbed her hand.

I turned hearing everyone else come out and we pulled out the herbs and bread we'd brought with us and went our ways to relieve ourselves before continuing our journey.

Through the woods, the thick trees and waters we continued for two days. At first, we heard nothing and then dogs, hound dogs, barking and getting closer to us as we ran through the woods.

I could see a swamp up ahead as we ran, meaning we were close, there was a home we were to hide in before we would make it to the ferry. They were afraid, afraid of getting caught. You could see the panic, clearly in their eyes. Abagail was running alongside of me when I grabbed her arm to stop her.

"Go, take them to the swamp and stay there hidden until I come. Take this just in case," I handed her the paper that was showing us the way. She took it, hugged me tightly and ran to catch up with the others.

I could hear the dogs and now horses, galloping nearby. I looked around trying to figure out my next move, but I saw nothing. Wait! Element of surprise, I thought and begin looking for a tree to climb. I quickly found the perfect one and headed up, it took all of five minutes for the dogs and the men to reach me. I'd already positioned myself and on the tree with an arrow and waited for the perfect shot. One dog stopped, circling each tree I'd touched before going to the next, the other, followed the trail to the swamps.

I wasn't worried. I'd informed Isaac if the dogs approached the water to pull it under and stab it. That way the only sound would be a splash, the owners would think the dog fell in. Two men on horses with raffles and one dog. I didn't have a gun, but due to my father teaching me how to shoot an arrow, I was an excellent marksman, so as I sat quietly, I had my arrow, ready. The bow crafted from wood, string from a piece of clothing which left little room to pull the arrow back which was crafted from wood and rocks.

I steadied my arrow as they circled on their horses. I took a deep breath and let go. The arrow connected to the first man forehead, right between his eyes and he fell off his horse.

"John! John!" The second man said now scared. I readied my second arrow for him and connected with his forehead just the same. The dog barked and since I was only able to make two arrows, I would have to fight with the sharpened spoons.

I slowly climbed down the tree with the dog nowhere in sight but once I reached the ground, the dog grabbed me by leg and begin dragging me away from the tree. It let go briefly only to grab ahold to my stomach, the pain was excruciating as I tried to ignore it and reach for one of the sharpen spoons. I couldn't scream, couldn't cry, I didn't have time. When it finally let go and tried to go for my face, I shoved the spoon through the roof of its mouth, killing it instantly.

It fell along side of me, and I just laid there breathing heavily, tired from wresting with the dog and in so much pain.

"Oh no," I heard as Isaac came near. My breathing was unsteady, but I was very alert. "You have to get up Ruth." He demanded pulling on me and I grunted in pain.

"I need to rest," I responded, out of breath.

"You can't, there's no time, we must keep moving. You said so."

I stared at him for a moment and then nodded my head in agreement.

He grabbed my right arm and placed it over his shoulder, allowing my weight to fall on him. The left side of my stomach and leg contained torn flesh. I could feel the tares on my flesh with every movement.

"Ruth!" MaryAnn said running to my aid. She examined my wombs, and quickly acted, cutting my pants leg and using it to wrap my leg, then lifting my shirt and binding my stomach and back the same. All I felt was agony, as I held a piece of cloth in my mouth to stop my screams.

Once I was all wrapped up, Isaac stood me up and we walked toward the swamp, the dirty muddy water I had to walk through with open wounds. I paused, I knew if I entered the water and infection would set in, a deadly one, but I made a promise and I was going to keep that promise. I saw them look at each other with worry but I keep moving, leaning on Isaac and MaryAnn as much as I could as we walked through the swamps. It wasn't too deep at first, it came up to our knees and then we were neck deep in the water.

We walked for what felt like days, pushing through the muddy, thick water until we made it to land. We stopped for a moment then walked two more miles. Night approached as we made it our next stop.

They were now practically dragging me as we came about fifteen feet from the front door. Before we could get any closer a Caucasian woman came out on the porch, speaking in a whisper. She stood there in her night gown, dirty blonde hair flowing a little past her shoulder. From what I could see, she was in her forties maybe fifties.

"How many are there of you?" She asked.

"Eight ma'am" MaryAnn responded.

"What's wrong with that one?"

"She was wounded by a dog; she just needs rest"

"No."

"Please ma'am."

"If she cannot stand up straight and walk in here on her own, I cannot help you, I will not risk it."

MaryAnn looked me and Isaac in dismay, but I fixed my eyes on the woman. Still with my breathing out of sorts, I straightened my leg slowly. Then removed my arm from Isaac's shoulder, placing all my weight on my right side. I placed my right hand over the stomach wound for support. I stood there, with all my might, all my strength, all that I am and looked her right in her eyes.

"Fine, come in," she said turning away and walking into the house right before I collapsed in Isaac's arms.

"My brave daughter," Isaac said before kissing my forehead.

I didn't feel brave at all, just tired and weak but I knew I had to be strong, strong for them. They were counting on me to see them to freedom, and I didn't want to let them down.

I was carried into the house, into the front room where there was a secret latch on the floor. She told the rest of us to get in while MaryAnn and Abigal stayed in the kitchen to get food for us all.

It was a crawl space, most people without a basement in my time had them. As I laid there on my back still trying to catch my breath, I could feel the pain slowly leaving my body.

"Everything said must be in a whisper and we must listen before speaking. Abagail went to bathe as the woman of house doesn't want the smell of us to linger, we are each to bathe. Women inside, men outside. How is she Papa?" MaryAnn asked but I didn't hear a response. I felt her hand grab mines as she came closer. "You did it! You got us out. Now we must go to the ferry in the morning" she said kissing the back of my hand.

"You must go…to the ferry…you must…wrap me up and allow me to sail with you…on the water" I responded. I was winded in between words.

"No, I won't leave you."

"You must…I'm okay…the pain…it's doesn't hurt as much. It's time…for you to go…to freedom…time…for me to go…home. I will sail…beside you…as you sail to freedom." MaryAnn kissed my forehead and placed her hand on the side of my face.

"Until we meet again," she said before softly singing, "I'm sorry, I'm gonna leave you"

The others softly sang in the background, "farewell, oh farewell."

"But I'll meet you in the morning."

"Farewell, oh farewell."

"I'll meeting you in the morning, I'm bound for the Promised Land, On the other side of Jordan, bound for the promised land."

Those were the last words I heard as I felt my last breath leave my body and I began floating. Watching as they grieved over me, men holding their hats against their chest, MaryAnn as she placed both of my hands in a cross on my chest.

I wanted to make sure they made it, I wanted to see them make it, but this was as far as I got. I hope they got farther.

Discovery

"Jewel! Jewel!" I heard someone calling my name. I jerked awake with a gasp and choking right after. "Are you okay? Jewel?" I heard and looked in the direction of the person calling my name. My given name. Aurora was there, sitting on the bed with concern in her eyes. I was home. Back in my time, back in my bed. "Jewel," she said once more.

"I'm fine, I just need some water." I responded, still a little winded.

"Ok" she responded and left the room.

I sat up on the bed rubbing the back of my neck trying to understand and comprehend what just happened. Was it a dream or something more?

"Here you go." Aurora said returning with a bottled water.

"Thank you," I replied before glopping the water down.

"Slow down. Did you turn into a fish or something while you were asleep? What were you dreaming about anyway, you scared me half to death, especially when I couldn't wake you."

"What's today?"

"Saturday," she said slowly. "Did you hit your head last night or something?"

"Saturday as in, the day after my birthday?"

"Yes," she said slowly again.

"Stop answering me like I'm crazy."

"Well, I wouldn't if I was sure, you weren't."

"Thank you for the water Aurora, I'm fine, you can go back to sleep."

"Sleep? It's 8 o'clock in the morning, sleep won't happen again until tonight, besides, it's still your birthday as far as I'm concerned, we have more fun planned."

"Yay," I said with sarcasm.

"Well don't sound so chipper about it." she said as she walked out the room.

I wasn't up nonsense today. I was more concerned about the dream I'd just had. Was it real or did I just have a crazy vivid nightmare.

I got up from my bed and walked into my bathroom. Grabbing the face towel, I turned on the faucet and begin cleaning my face. The closer I looked into the mirror the more I saw Ruth. She was right there, not next to me but she was…me. Standing tall, strong, and determined. I could clearly see her scars, those physical and mental. Then I remembered, the dog bites on her left side. I slowly lifted my shirt to see if there were scars from the trauma, I'd experienced in my dream but there were none. However, the spots, the small beauty marks were there. I've always wondered about them. You could barely see them unless you pointed them out because their color was so close to my skin tone.

"They're in the same spots," I softly said aloud. The exact same spots the dog bit Ruth, how is that possible? Is Ruth an ancestor, part of a family line I never knew about, and her wounds passed down to me or was Ruth…me?

I shook my head at the thought because that is impossible, right? Has to be, I thought and hung that rag up and begin to moisturize my face. I don't know if it was the moisturizer but a small spark, a small glow came over my face, hope maybe.

I walked back to my bed and climbed in, pulling the covers over me but I couldn't, or my mind wouldn't let me shake the feeling. Maybe I needed to know, if what I dreamt was real. Did they make it? Did they keep going? I needed to know, so I grabbed my laptop and powered it on.

"Hey sis, look what I got." Amariah said walking into my room with bags in her hands. She was shaking them with excitement, so I knew exactly what it was. We both said, "food" at the same time. "I got you all your fixings, and a breakfast fav."

"What breakfast fav?" I asked, as I watched her sat the bags down and take the food containers out.

"Rice of course! I never understood, you and Dad's fascination with rice for breakfast."

"Genetics, thank you." I said snatching a small brown paper bag out of her hand before she could place it on my nightstand. I looked inside and pulled out a small bowl of rice. "Yes!" I said in excitement.

"You're a strange one sister," she said shaking her head.

"Thank you."

"Not a compliment. Any who, did you have anything in

particular, you'd like to do today?"

"Um, research, I had a crazy dream, and it has inspired me to look up a few things" I said eating a spoon full of rice. She had it made just like I like it, butter and cheese.

"Do you want to talk about it?"

"No."

"Um okay, and what are you doing after that?"

"Hm, I don't know?"

"What about a nice quiet dinner? Oh, Oh and maybe a spa day?"

"How are you going to book a spa this late?"

"I have connections, all you have to do is say yes." she said with a smile. The way she looked at me, she was so excited, how could I say no.

"Fine!"

"Yes! Okay, spa than dinner after, I'm going to go book it right now" she was giddy per usual as she left the room.

I took a long sigh after she left. Celebrating with my sisters was not really the problem. Celebrating without my father was, not having that piece of me weighed heavy. No more dad jokes, no more stories from his childhood or how him and Mom met, he was gone. The one thing I thought about the most was, my mother was still young, only in her 50s, she no longer had her husband to grow old with, she was now taking this journey alone.

I shook my head, shaking off the pain I felt and the tears that were beginning to form in my eyes. I needed to focus, focus on finding the truth behind my dream. Question is; where do I start?

After I finished my breakfast, I continued my search. I typed in Slave names, Slave ferries, people who escaped to freedom and all came up short. Then I remembered Harriet Tubman or Minty then, she was the reason we escaped, the main source. If I traced her steps; maybe I can find them.

At first, nothing came about it and then; for some strange reason, the state Pennsylvania stood out to me. I doubt it I would be able to find the ferry but records, yes maybe they are records of their arrival.

I searched for two hours, for Pennsylvania slave records and found nothing and then Harriet Tubman freedom papers and that too was a dead end. I threw my notebook across the room in frustration as Aurora walked in.

"See this is why a spa is needed. Wait, why aren't you dressed?" She asked.

"I've been in here doing some research."

"The entire time! Jewel, our spa appointment is in an hour."

"Okay, okay, just let me finish…"

"No," she said closing my laptop. "Trust me the research that you're doing will still be there when we get back. You need some me time and by the looks of it, you need to relax."

"Fine, I'll get ready."

"Great!" she said taking my laptop off the bed and placing it under her arm.

"Hey! What are you doing?"

"Oh, yeah, see I don't trust your response so, if you don't have your laptop, you have no excuse to not get ready."

"Really Aurora?"

"Yes, a nice trick I learned from Dad. Bye," she said waving me off as she exited the room.

"So annoying."

"I heard that!" she yelled from down the hall.

She was right though. I was so consumed with finding MaryAnn and everyone else that I forgot what I agreed to do with my sisters.

I let out a long sigh before getting up, showering and getting dressed.

Finally dressed in black cargo shorts, a red crop top and black sandals. I headed downstairs where I could hear my sisters laughing.

"What are you guys down here doing?" I asked coming around the corner. "Is that my shirt?" I asked Amariah.

"Yes, I borrowed it, I knew you wouldn't mind." She responded.

"Really Amariah, who told you that?"

"Oh relax, as many times as we watched you raid Mom and Dad's closet." I raised one of my eyebrows. "Aurora was too young to remember but I remember Dad was going out one night and he was looking for a particular green shirt to wear and he asked Mom about it. Well, she didn't know where it was and Jewel, you walked out of our room with it on and he saw you. I heard him say, 'Is that my shirt,' and I saw you slowly walk backward back into our room." She said laughing. I walked over to the dining room table where they were sitting.

"I guess you missed the part where Mom got up from the bed and I heard Dad ask her, 'Are those my shorts?' and she responded, 'No, these are our shorts.' We all started laughing.

"So, you're saying that borrowing clothes is learned behavior?" Aurora asked.

"Pretty much" I said, and we laughed again.

"Alright you two, enough of this, let's head to the spa, Sara should be on her way."

We grabbed our things and headed out. I didn't say much on the ride over, too sad, too hurt thinking about all the good times we had with our father. I didn't want to stay in this sunken place but climbing out seemed harder than staying there.

My mind drifted the whole ride over and up until we arrived and walked into the spa. The host presented us with a glass of champagne and led to room where we would have a group massage.

"Um, what kind of massage did you book us for?" I asked.

"Therapeutic, weren't you listening when she was describing everything?" Aurora asked.

"When…when did she do that?" I asked.

"Okay, clearly this is needed, so just relax. Everything is

covered, we are all here with you. Just try to relax," she said softly. I was making my sister's worry; I didn't want that. In response, I shook my head in the yes motion and prepared for my massage.

Aurora was right, it was exactly what I needed. From the full body massage, the Medi and Pedi, the facial and then relaxing in the jacuzzi after was everything. We talked and laughed the entire time making me completely forget about my grief.

"You guys, it's getting late and have dinner plans at eight remember." Amariah said.

"Right, let's make our way home," said Aurora.

"Home? We're not going out to eat?" I asked.

"No, Mom hired a private chef to come over, so we can just relax at home," said Amariah.

"Alright, let's get to it," Sara said getting out of the jacuzzi with her empty champagne glass.

"Sara are you okay, I see you finished your glass?" I asked.

"Girl, I'm good, I'm no lightweight. I am ready to eat though" she responded, and we laughed.

After we got dressed, we headed back to the house to prepare for dinner.

I don't know when they did it but there were pajamas on my bed with a note, "for dinner tonight" guess that meant we all had the same ones. I rolled my eyes. I guess I shouldn't complain too much they were a rose gold shirt and short set. Silk? Is this silk? I said in my head as I touched the fabric. That must have been Amariah's doing, if you let her, she will splurge on clothes and jewelry for sure. I shook my head. She still had my laptop, and I was sure she had no plans on returning it until after dinner.

"Jewel, hurry up," Sara yelled from downstairs. I could smell the food cooking which means so was the chef.

"I'm coming," I yelled back and headed downstairs. As I cut the corner, I saw Sara and my sisters sitting at the island in the kitchen, all with wine glasses. There were two men tending to the food on the stove, both with their backs turned towards me. Sara gestured for me to sit down on the empty stool next to her.

"Best friend!" She said, hugging me as I sat down.

"So, how much did she have to drink?" I asked.

"Just a glass, I didn't want to give her too much before dinner was ready." The taller man said as he turned around with a smile. "Hi, I'm Ryan and this is my assistant Ian. I'm assuming you're the birthday girl," he said.

"You would assume correct," I responded to this man, this

very handsome darkskin man with a white smile, perfect fade, muscular shape body, and intriguing voice. I was in a trance but snapped out of it when he looked away to finish preparing the meal. When I looked at my sisters, they were smirking at me.

"What?" I asked.

"Nothing," they both said and looked away.

Ryan turned back towards me sliding me a glass of wine.

"So, I'm told you like seafood," he said.

"Correct again."

"Well let me start the meal off with mini crab cakes with a drizzle of Remoulade sauce." He said stepping back from the island as Ian placed small plates in front of us that contained two small crabs, one in the center of the plate and other slightly hanging off the side of the other, with a small fork on the side.

"Thank you," I said before tasting the food. "Wow, this, this is amazing. Is this your recipe?"

"Yes, and thank you for the compliment."

"You're welcome." I said covering my mouth because at that point I was eating faster.

"I wouldn't eat so fast. You tend to swallow air and I would like for you to leave room for the entrée as well as dessert." He said and I heard someone's fork hit their plate.

I cleared my throat, covering my mouth before saying, "My apology, guess I was hungrier than I thought."

"No apologies necessary, it's a compliment when others enjoy my cooking." He smiled then turned around to finish cooking the rest of the meal and I turn to look at everyone else who was side eyeing me as they ate.

"Really," I said to them, leaning my head to the side.

"I'm just saying," said Sara and she straighten herself in her seat and took another sip of her wine, wide-eyed.

I turned a shook my head. I knew what they were doing, and I knew what they were getting at. I was single and had been for years now. I kind of preferred it that way. It was less of a hassle worrying about someone else.

"So, Ryan, how long have you been a chief?" Aurora asked. Ryan turned around and looked at Aurora.

"About five years now, I like to keep it simple. Small staff, private dinners, weddings, it's easier to engage with clients," he said.

Before Aurora can ask another question, Ian turned around and placed a salad in front of her as he removed her plate from the crab cakes.

"This is Ryan's signature salad, very leafy, thin sliced chicken, slightly roasted tomatoes, feta cheese, with olives and chips on the side" Ian said. Ian was very handsome as well, a little smaller than Ryan but still muscular, more of a caramel complexion and a nice haircut.

"What about the dressing?" asked Aurora.

"According to your mother, you all love ranch dressing. The dressing has been tossed into the salad, not too much, not too little." Aurora nodded as she dug into her salad. Ryan removed all our plates before Ian served us salad.

I watched as they placed the plates in the sink and begin to clean and dry them. Ryan walked over the oven that was built into the wall and checked on our entrée.

"Do you mind telling us what entrée we have the pleasure of tasting?" I asked.

"Element of surprise," he said with a smile.

Amariah stopped eating, put her elbows on the table and rested her chin on them. "So, have you ever just been a private chief for a family or a person, say, a single…woman?" She asked.

Ryan laughed before responding. "I have, but it didn't last long."

"Oh, may I ask what transpired?"

"Um, she wanted something, she could not have." Amariah's

eyebrow went up. She was intrigued, I on the other hand was annoyed.

"Let's keep it professional ladies," I said eyeing them before taking another sip of my wine.

"Harmless fun," Ryan said.

"Oh, you have no idea." he laughed and turned around to help Ian finish cleaning.

"Ladies, is it okay if I use your bathroom?" Ian asked.

"Sure, it's down the hall, I'll show you," Aurora said as she gestured him to follow her.

Ryan turned the fire down on the stove and threw the rag he had over his shoulder before turning around and asking, "So, how do you all like the food so far?"

"So good." Amariah said with a mouthful.

"Amazing," said Sara.

"And you, Jewel, are you enjoying your meal?"

"I am, it's really good." I said in a low voice. Ryan took a step back and folded his arms.

"Are you okay?" I asked.

"Fine, probably should have told Ian to make it quick, as I have to utilize the bathroom as well."

"Oh."

"Jewel has one upstairs…in her room." Sara said, and I side eyed her instantly.

"Oh no, I wouldn't want to make you feel uncomfortable" Ryan responded and now I felt bad. I peeked around the corner hoping Ian and Aurora would return but only Aurora came back and sat back in her seat.

"It's fine Ryan, I can show you," I said.

"Are you sure?"

"Yes, come on" I gestured and led him upstairs. "The bathroom is right there." I pointed as I stood at my bedroom door.

"Thank you."

"No problem." I said lowering my head and looking at the floor as he passed by me. I looked over and noticed my laptop sitting on my bed. Aurora must have put it back after showing Ian the bathroom downstairs.

I walked over to my bed and picked it up. I was too eager to continue my research. When I opened it, Aurora had left a yellow sticky note on the screen that read, "not until after dinner." Great! I slammed the laptop shut and threw it on the bed, placing my hands on my hips in frustration. I hadn't even noticed that Ryan was watching me.

"Hey, are you okay?" he asked.

"Um, yes I'm fine," I said rubbing my forehead.

"Okay because I thought you were getting ready to go to war with your laptop."

"No, I just…I've been researching something and I'm having a hard time finding what I'm looking for and I promised my sister I wouldn't look more until after dinner but I'm…I'm just…I don't know."

"I can assist, if you need it?" He said stepping closer.

"No, no thank you Ryan, I really don't want to make a big deal out of it, just want to enjoy dinner."

"Seems like it's already a big deal."

"I'm fine…" I begin to say as I turned toward Ryan who was now six feet away from me. "Um, let's forget about it, I'm excited to taste the entrée you've prepared."

"Okay, ladies first." he said extending his arm to the door.

When we arrived back downstairs everyone was laughing and talking, the salads were cleared, and Ian was now placing a new dish in front of us. He served everyone except for me. Ryan said he'd created this tradition in which he would serve the special guest himself.

"Roasted salmon over rice, with garlic green beans, with slight honey drizzle and almond bites." Ryan said.

"My favorite," I said.

"According to your Mom, yes," Ryan said with a smile handing me my fork.

"Thank you," I smiled back.

"Oh, so you do have teeth," another half-smile emerged, and I looked at him but didn't respond. Instead, I dig into my food which tasted amazing. I felt like I was floating on a cloud.

We sat and continued our meal, laughing and joking. I engaged as well however I couldn't help but think about MaryAnn, I needed to know. Needed to know if they were safe.

"Well ladies, thank you all for having us, I truly appreciate this opportunity and it was really fun getting to know you all" Ryan said.

"Aww don't leave, we're having so much fun," said Amariah.

"We don't want to intrude; we like to do our job and leave you full and satisfied."

"Okay, well it was great meeting you both" I heard her say and then my mind drifted. Thinking about my laptop again.

"Still thinking about research, I see," Ryan said softly. "You know I can help you; I don't mind."

"How do you know if you can even help?" I asked.

"How do you know I can't? What are you researching?" I looked at everyone else, too engaged in their conversation to pay us any mind.

"I am looking for records, records of slaves that escaped to freedom, particular ones."

"Have you tried the Pennsylvania Anti-Slavery Society?"

"No, would that have been the one Harriet Tubman traveled too?"

"Yes, where she changed her name from Minty to Harriet, where William Still assisted her."

"Hm, I think you may be of help after all."

"Okay well let's get to it!" He said rubbing his hands together. "How about you grab your laptop, while I pack up things."

"Sounds like plan," I said smiling, I placed my wine glass down and headed upstairs to grab my laptop.

With my laptop in hand, I came back downstairs and notice Sara grabbing her things.

"Oh no, are you leaving?" I asked.

"Yes, I have a lot to do tomorrow, and I have to get an early start." I smiled and raised my arms to hug her.

"Thank you for spending this time with me."

"No problem, friend, but I need you to fight."

"What do you mean?"

"Fight the pain, fight the hurt and not let it overwhelm you. You are strong and always have been. You don't see it now, but you will." I smiled and she hugged me once more. "I love you and we'll talk soon. Love you girls, have a good night!" she yelled back at my sisters before leaving.

As she was walking out, Ryan was walking back in.

"Is she leaving?" He asked.

"Yes."

"Okay, I'll be right back." He said leaving back out.

I stood in the doorway, waiting. During the goodbyes, I watched as Ian cleaned the entire kitchen, no dirty dish or countertop left behind. When I turned back around Ryan was on his way back in the house.

"Is everything okay?" I asked.

"Oh yes, I was just making sure she got to her car and pulled off safely."

"Okay."

"Shall we," he said with a hand gesture.

"We shall," I responded leaded him to the living room where

everyone was.

"Here you two, since they packed up all their dishes, I pulled out some wine glasses and wine for you." Amairah said pointing to the glasses and wine on the living room table. "I on the other hand, I'm going to bed."

"Already?" Aurora protested.

"Yes, you know I'm not a night owl, I've had my fun. Thank you for the food, it was nice meeting you both and goodnight." She said and headed up to her room.

"And then there were four." I said before sitting on the couch. Ian and Aurora smiled at me then continued their conversation. They kept their voices low, I guess it was private. Ryan sat down next to me and poured us both a glass.

"So, shall we start?" He asked.

"Yes" I placed my laptop on my lap and opened it, pulling up a web search and typing in, Pennsylvania Anti-Slavery Society. "Since this was your idea…would you mind?" I asked handing him the laptop.

"Not at all," putting his glass down he began scrolling the web. "Do you have a timeframe, names of these individuals?"

"Names changed when they arrived to freedom didn't they? Do you think they would have the name they were given before that?"

"Of course, maybe a little difficult but with time, I'm sure we can find information on them."

"Okay, as for the timeframe, it would be between maybe 1850 and 1860."

"A ten-year gap maybe difficult to achieve." I looked away with sadness. "But not impossible, are you sure about the dates?"

"Yes, Harriet Tubman escaped in 1849 and she waited a year before going back to retrieve her family. The people I'm looking for, would have been slaves that Harriet helped, ones she gave a map to."

"You know she helped a lot of slaves?"

"I do but..." I sighed. "You think I'm wasting my time, don't you?"

"No not at all, there are many records but I'm sure we can narrow it down."

His reassurance was what I needed and when I smiled at him, he knew it. I needed to see if the dream I had was real, to see, if they were real.

I had to get a little closer to him so that we could both see the screen and after an hour we found several books that contained the names of escaped slaves. The pages were uploaded to the web, yellow and some torn but contained information all the same. We strolled through them page by page reading all it contained.

"Didn't you say one name was Issac?" Ryan asked.

"Yes, where are you looking?" I asked.

"Here." he pointed. "Says, Father Issac and daughter MaryAnn arrived fall of 1851 with five others. One left behind, deceased, left on the water." I gasped, covering my mouth and unconsciously spilling my wine on my shirt.

"Oh," I said, the front of my shirt now soaked. Ryan jumped up around and when into the kitchen. He came back with a damp cloth and baking soda.

"Here, if you dab it out fast, it won't stain," he said handing me the cloth and baking soda.

"Thank you," I said and took my shirt off, I was wearing another under it.

"You're welcome." Ryan sat back down next to me. "That information must have startled you. Was it correct? Were those the individuals you were looking for?"

"Yes, I, I apologize for..."

"No, don't apologize, we all have our movements, it's what we do with them after." I nodded in agreement.

"I just, this is going to sound crazy."

"Try me."

"I had the strangest dream that, I was slave and those people, they were my family. And I…" I hesitated. "I…"

"You don't have to tell me all of it, but I do believe we have spiritual connection to our ancestors. Like that necklace you have on for intense. It looks like ancient treasure." I placed my hand over it.

"Yes, my mother gave it to me for my birthday."

"A symbol and strong reminded of who you are."

"Why…why do you say that?"

"It's the same for my family. I know a lot of families don't have a lot passed down jewels from their ancestors, but my father is an archeologist. After tracing our history, we stumbled across some treasures that belong to our ancestors and were able to keep a few. Mostly from men in the family. When I see such jewelry, I'm drawn to it. Make sure to keep it in the family, its precious."

"Very interesting to know."

"I'm a man of many talents including honor and since we've found your missing ancestors, I will take my leave." I laughed.

"You sound ancient yourself."

"I know, I don't know why, maybe it's hereditary," he said

shrugging his shoulders and I smiled.

"It is pretty late, and it seems, those two are pretty tired." I pointed to Aurora and Ian who'd fallen asleep in each other arms.

"Indeed," Ryan stood up and walked over to Ian, hitting Ian's leg with the back of his hand. Ian opened his eyes and Ryan gestured that he was ready to go.

Ian looked down at Aurora still asleep on his shoulder and slowly moved away, laying her softly on the couch.

"Don't worry, I got her," I whispered.

They both tiptoed toward the door after grabbing the rest of their things. I waved at Ian, and he sleepily walked to their truck.

"Thank you for having me." Ryan said standing in the doorway. I was leaning on the open door.

"Thank you for coming and for the food, it was amazing."

"Well, if you ever need a chief or research partner again, give me call." Ryan handed me his card.

"Will do, be safe." I said and he gave me a smile before headed to his truck. I gave one more wave before they drove off and I closed and locked the door.

"Well, that was interesting?" Aurora said through a yawn.

"You mean you and Ian, aww so cute." I teased.

"Actually, I mean you and Ryan." she said as she walked past me.

"Funny."

"No, not funny…. interesting."

"Goodnight Aurora," I said as she walked up the stairs to her room.

"Hey, I'm just saying."

I shook my head and went to the couch and cleaned up the wine and glasses we used, then grabbed my laptop and headed up to bed.

It was a good night, great food, conversation and fun. I guess I really did enjoy my birthday and tomorrow I get to just relax.

After climbing into my bed, I tried to remove the necklace once more and again it didn't budge. So, I laid down, took a couple breaths, relaxed my body and drifted off to sleep. I'd worry about the necklace in the morning.

Confirmation

I went to sleep, hoping I wouldn't jump anymore timelines and thankfully I didn't. However, I did dream, dreamt that I was in a room. I stood there looking up, down and around and behind me there was a mirror. I looked in it, a different version of myself looked back. I was in a dusty dress, just like the one MaryAnn wore.

Wait! Am I looking at Ruth? I asked myself, as I slowing walked towards the mirror. My reflection smiled, not a scary smile but a warm one. I guess to let me know that everything was okay. Behind her, two other versions of me walked up behind her, one was dressed as if she were royalty with a golden headpiece, black beaded hair and wrapped dress. She looked Egyptian. Before I could get a good look at the other one more came and words begin to form on the mirror. I stepped back to read them.

"You are. You are, you are…" were the words that appeared on the mirror as the women spoke to them as well.

"You are… strength! You are kind! Love! Ambition! Leader! Queen! Fighter! Warrior! Inspiration! Unbreakable! Powerful! You are….us and we are you" They said the last part in unison.

What was this? I didn't know what was happening but the encouragement, the support made me feel…. seen, heard and understood.

I walked up to the mirror and placed my hand on it, Ruth, connected hers to mines and smiled once more before I woke up out of my sleep. I was in my room, still in my own time. I looked over the clock on my dresser and it was 4:02 am, was a coincidence, the exact time I was born.

I turned back overlooking up at the ceiling. I somehow felt relieved, as if a weight had been lifted off my shoulders. I yawled, curled up on my side to go back to sleep and felt something cold in my bed. I sat up, grabbed it realizing it was the necklace, the one I could not get off last night, had fallen off on its own. I picked it up and examined it before placing it on my dresser. It was weird, weirdest thing I had experienced but I still felt grateful. Without hesitation I laid down and drifted off to a peaceful sleep.

The next morning, I couldn't wait to talk to my mother to tell her everything that happened.

"Hey sweets, how was your weekend?" She asked.

"Well, I had quite the adventure" she laughed.

"I bet you did, and you don't have to tell me what happened, but I want to know did you get the message?"

"I believe so."

"Well, if you didn't, let me tell you this. That journey was to show you that the same person that you were then, you are the same person now. So, if you were strong then, you are strong now and if you were brave then, you are brave now. You wanted to know who you are and now you were shown. I want you to know that you will always be those things. No matter if you are sad, angry or hurt. Those traits are embedded into your soul."

"That's…" I said holding back my tears. "Something I really needed to hear, really needed to know."

"Now you do and it's up to you what you do with that information."

"Yes ma'am."

"Well alright, I'm going to get off and finished cooking breakfast. Why don't you go downstairs and grab something to eat as well. I sent a gift over for you."

"Another one?"

"Yes, it's a good one too."

"Alright Mom, I'll talk to you later. I love you."

"I love you too."

After I sat my phone down, I took one last look in the mirror before heading downstairs. I was still in my pajamas when I walked into the kitchen and saw Ryan and Ian sitting at the kitchen table.

Ryan cleared his throat when he saw me and jumped up

from the table.

"Um, what's going on?" I asked.

"Mom sent Ryan and Ian over to make breakfast for us" Aurora said with a smile.

"Oh." I responded.

"I hope that's okay?" Ryan asked.

"Um…of course. So…what did you make?" I asked looking around. Ryan stood up and pulled out the empty chair next to him.

"Come, sit down. I'll make your plate."

"Alright." I responded and walked over. I joined in on the conversation with my sisters and Ian while Ryan prepared my plate.

This felt good, like old friends hanging out.

"Thank you." I said to Ryan when he sat the plate in front of me. "You know if you two are going to keep coming around like this, we might have to charge you rent." Everyone laughed. "I don't know what it is, but it feels like we've all known each other for a long time or have met before," Ryan said staring into my eyes.

"Hmm, maybe we have." I smiled and ate a piece of my pancake. Ryan laughed and we continued talking amongst each other.

This was different, this was what I needed. Hope and reassurance and frankly I'm glad I got down to the root of matter because now; now I understand me. I feel like, I can be the best version of myself. Now I know, who I am, and I was always meant to be.

ABOUT THE AUTHOR

Root of the Matter

Sharnnell Spivey was born and raised in Detroit, Michigan where she first realized her passion for writing. She became an author at the age of 15 and continues to write Novels on current topics with the intent to inspire others.

The one thing she wants when she writes, is her work to have a positive message in it.

Something people can hold onto, hope.

Root of the Matter

Made in the USA
Columbia, SC
21 March 2025